While Walking To The Cross

Patricia R. Frank

While Walking To The Cross
ISBN 9781645383383

"While walking to the cross"…with Jesus, we take that bitter journey while we stop to eat, to pray, to betray and deny, to protest, to carry our crosses, and to hear.

Through that journey, we truly experience the agony and the suffering that Jesus endured from the Passover Feast, into the Garden of Gethsemane, then during the endless night of being brutally beaten and scourged, and finally being put to death in the most despicable manner of that era; crucifixion.

So let's walk together during this Lenten season, always, keeping in mind the glorious victory won by Christ revealed in His Resurrection.

That is why we exclaim:
"He is risen, He is risen indeed; Alleluia!
When our Easter includes the celebration of our Lord
and Savior's glorious Resurrection, then we
TRULY KNOW ABOUT EASTER!

When we don't walk to the cross with Jesus, then Easter is just a time for 'worldly fun'; spring breaks from school, buying new spring clothes, buying candy to put in decorated baskets, and coloring hardboiled eggs; even though we call them 'Easter Eggs'.

The day is soon forgotten while we're still eating Jelly Beans, unwrapping candy eggs, and making egg salad from left over hardboiled eggs.

Table of Contents:

While We Come And Eat

The Lord's Supper Magnificently painted by Leonardo Da Vinci from 1495 to 1498 can be seen in Milan Italy. Can you believe painted In the Fifteenth Century when Christopher Columbus discovered American? Only four disciples were initially recognized in the original painting; Peter, James, John, and Judas. In the 19th Century notes were found in DaVinci's notebook, and the eight other disciples were named. There are various reproductions of the original painting, and some have the names of all twelve disciples written on the hem of the tablecloth, and so it is with the one shown. I took a photo of a print given to my Maternal Grandparents on their wedding day, March 27, 1910, and all the disciple's names are written on the hem of the tablecloth.

Jesus' twelve disciples seated from left are: Bartholomaus, Jacobus II, Andreas, Judas (holding the money bag), Petrus, Joannes, Center is Jesus Christus, Thomas, Jacobus I, Philippus, Matthaus, Thaddeus, and Simon.

Jesus' disciples didn't know about Easter yet, when Jesus asked them to find a place to celebrate the Passover. All the disciples knew at this time was that Jesus, and they, being Jews were following in the Jewish Tradition of celebrating the Passover which commemorated the Passover in Egypt when the Children of Israel were Pharaoh's slaves. Pharaoh being obstinate in honoring Moses' request to free the Children of Israel caused God to intervene very harshly for the last time.

And we remember from The Old Testament that God instructed Moses to tell the Children of Israel to sacrifice a young unblemished male lamb, and to paint the blood of the lamb on the two doorposts, and on the lintels of their homes. God promised in executing judgement, that He would pass over Egypt, and strike down all the first born in the land of Egypt, both man and beast. The lamb's blood on the homes of the Children of Israel would save them from God's Promise of destruction toward Egypt and Pharaoh himself. The Jewish People celebrate that 'Passover in Egypt' to this very day.

In Luke 22:7-20 we are told how Jesus instructed the disciples in regard to finding the Upper Room and preparing for the Passover. Jesus sent Peter and John saying: "Go and prepare the Passover for us, that we may eat it." And the disciples asked Jesus where He wanted them to prepare it. Jesus told them: "Behold, when you have entered the city, a man will meet you carrying a pitcher of water; follow him into the house that he enters. You will say to the owner of the house, "The Teacher says to you, "Where is the guest room in which I may eat the Passover with my disciples?" "He will show you a large furnished upper room; prepare the Passover there." The disciples went and found everything just as Jesus had told them, and they prepared the Passover.

And so, the disciples did not know as they were seated at the table with Jesus that Jesus was to become another unblemished lamb, but now would be THE LAMB OF GOD whose blood would be shed on a cross by tomorrow afternoon.

And Jesus being THE LAMB OF GOD was the significance of Jesus instituting The Lord's Supper, which now signified that His blood would become the very blood of a slain unblemished lamb that would save mankind, and Jesus would, again, fulfill the prophesies of the Old Testament; especially as we read Isaiah 53. All the disciples even Judas had been invited to The Lord's Supper. Did the disciples wonder about 'this being a different kind of a 'Passover'. This was obvious different from the Passovers they had celebrated in the past especially as they watched Jesus bless the bread, and say, "Take and eat, this is My body which is given for you; do this in remembrance of Me." After the same manner Jesus took the cup, and after He had blessed it, He said, "This cup which is poured out for you is the new covenant in My blood which is shed for you; do this in remembrance of Me."

Jesus invites us to His table, and a clergy cannot deny anyone The Sacrament of Holy Communion, because Jesus denies no one. Jesus certainly did not deny Judas. Jesus' statement at the table: "One of you will betray Me", troubled the disciples, and they started to ask, "Is It I?" "Is it I Lord?" Jesus replied, "The one who I have offered some bread to", and it was Judas. Jesus only commented to Judas, "What you are going to do, do quickly." With that Judas left the room. Jesus did, of course, know what Judas had planned.

The clergy has been ordained to bless and administer the bread and wine, and the clergy expresses Jesus' words: "Take and eat, this is My body given for you. Do this in remembrance of Me. This is My blood shed for you. Do this in remembrance of Me".

Only we can examine ourselves, confess and can be truly sorry for our sins of thoughts, words, and deeds. Then we can come humbly and unworthily to the Lord's Table in penitence, seeking God's mercy and forgiveness. We can confess as the publican in the temple, not even being able to look up toward heaven, but looking down and beating his chest, and saying: "God, be merciful to me a sinner." A clergy can declare forgiveness, but only the Lord can see true penitence in a person's heart, and whether forgiveness will be granted.

Receiving the Sacrament of Holy Communion is a truly beautiful way of witnessing our faith; and that is by believing that our Lord and Savior Jesus Christ is truly present in the bread and wine which we are about to receive.

And, as we leave the 'table' with our faith having been nourished and strengthened; we thank God for this gift and reflect on God's forgiveness and abiding love.

Beautiful words from a hymn,
"Lord may Thy body and Thy blood.
Be for my soul the highest good".

While We Pray

Why do we pray? How should we pray? When should we pray? Where should we pray? What should we pray for?

On the Internet there are numerous links with possibly over 1,000 books on prayer, and ranging in prices from $6.49 to $28.51. There probably are countless more books on prayer in every bookstore, and I certainly believe that The Holy Spirit has inspired many authors in a sincere effort to help and enrich the prayer life of their readers.

As the disciples went with Jesus to the Garden of Gethsemane, Jesus said" Sit here until I have prayed". Then Jesus took Peter, James, and John further into the garden, and said to them: "My soul is deeply grieved to the point of death; remain here and keep watch." Jesus went on by Himself to pray. The disciples failed to remember that Jesus had told them that He would suffer, would die, and would rise in three days, and yet tonight they didn't consider anything out of the ordinary, because Jesus had on several occasions gone off by Himself to pray. We read He had gone up a mountain, and on other occasions we read that He just went off by Himself to pray.

But tonight was very different! Jesus prayed: "Father, if Thou art willing, remove this cup from Me; yet not My will, but Thine be done."

The disciples, being human, got tired and fell asleep, and Jesus finding them asleep said to Peter: "Simon, are you asleep? Could you not watch with Me for one hour? Keep watching and praying that you may not come into temptation; the spirit is willing, but the flesh is weak."

Jesus left them, and went away again to pray, and an angel from heaven appeared to strengthen Him. Being in agony Jesus was praying very fervently, and His *sweat became like drops of blood falling down upon the ground. And a second time He returned, and found them sleeping for their eyes were heavy. Returning to pray, and finding them asleep for third time, Jesus said to them: "Are you still sleeping and taking your rest? It is enough; the hour has come; behold the Son of Man is being betrayed into the hands of sinners. Arise, let us be going; behold the one who betrays Me is at hand."

If we had gone to the garden with Jesus, would we have been tempted to fall asleep too? A sober hymn comes to mind, "Go To Dark Gethsemane, ye that feel the tempter's power. Your Redeemer's conflicts see; watch with Him one bitter hour. Turn not from His griefs away; learn of Jesus Christ to pray."

In Matthew chapter 6, Jesus' disciples asked Jesus to teach them to pray, and Jesus said: "When you pray, pray in this way", and Jesus taught them:

The Lord's Prayer
Our Father Who Art In Heaven; God wants us to believe that He is our true Father, and that we would come to Him as His dear children. We know how to go and speak to our earthly father, but how do we go to our Heavenly Father? Do we even think about having a Heavenly Father, and talking to Him in a prayerful manner? We know how to ask our earthly father for 'things', but how do we ask our Heavenly Father for 'what'? And, what would we ask Him for? Jesus tells us that God knows what we need even before we ask.

*Medical Term for sweating blood: Hematohidrosis is caused from extreme stress when blood leaks from intact skin appearing as beads of sweat.

Jesus tells us that when you pray, go into your inner room, and when you have shut the door, pray to your Father who is in secret, and your Father who sees in secret will repay you. For encouragement we read in Romans 8:26-28 "And in the same way the Holy Spirit also helps our weakness; for we do not know how to pray as we should, the Spirit Himself intercedes for us with groaning too deep for words. And God who searches the hearts knows what the mind of the Spirit is, because He intercedes for the saints according to the will of God". Jesus tells us in His Sermon on the Mount in Matthew 7:9-11 "Even an earthly father being sinful knows how to give good gifts to his children; how much more shall your Heavenly Father who is in heaven give what is good to those who ask Him."

Hallowed Be Thy Name; God's name is holy, and we should want to honor His name in a manner that is pleasing to Him. God has revealed Himself to us throughout Holy Scriptures, and we honor Him and His Holy name by leading godly lives according to God's Word.

God's name is also hallowed when His Word, the Bible, is taught in its truth and purity; when nothing is added to His Word or taken away from His Word. Our sincere faithfulness to God will be seen and will be evident in our actions and our deeds in the way we interact with others. In all we do and say, we give God the glory! In Matthew 15:8 we warned about: "This people honors Me with their lips, but their heart is far from Me." Let us never bring dishonor to God's holy name by taking His name in vain through cursing or swearing. It must sadden God deeply to hear His name used in anger or in common day-to-day language.

Thy Kingdom Come; It was through Pentecost that God gave the out-pouring of the Holy Spirit, and by that significant out-pouring by the Holy Spirit many were baptized and came to believe that through our Lord and Savior Jesus Christ, all have been redeemed and saved from sin, death, and the power of the devil. Through the power of the Holy Spirit and the Word of God the Kingdom of God comes to enrich, sanctifies, and reigns to keep us in the through faith. Not only in our lives, but we pray that the Kingdom of God will come and shine throughout the world in all lives, that all peoples may lead a godly live here on earth, and for eternity.

We are encouraged and empowered by the Holy Spirit to bring the Kingdom of God to others. In Jesus' Sermon On The Mound in Matthew 5:13-14 Jesus invites us to be "the salt of the earth" and "the light of the world". With our 'salting' and letting our 'lights' shine, we are witnesses to others by what we do and say bringing glory and honor to God.

Thy Will Be Done On Earth As It Is In Heaven; It is God's good and gracious will that all men be saved, and to come to the knowledge of truth. Jesus tells us in John 6:40 "It is the will of My Father, that everyone who beholds the Son and believes in Him, may have eternal life, and I Myself will raise him up on the last day." God's will can be done in us when we resist what we are warned about in 1 John 5:16 "Love not the world, neither the things that are in the world. If any man loves the world, the love of the Father is not in him. For all that is in the world, the lust of the flesh, and the lust of the eyes, and the pride of life is not of the Father, but is of the world." With the help of the Holy Spirit, our faith will be strengthened, and we will remain steadfast and abide in God's Holy will unto our earthly end.

Give Us This Day Our Daily Bread; We ask for daily bread, which also includes everything we need for our mortal bodies, and our very existence. This includes, food, clothing, home, and family. God gives us our 'daily bread' purely out of Fatherly divine goodness and mercy. In Psalm 145:15-16 we read "The eyes of all wait upon Thee, and Thou givest them their meat in due season. Thou openest Thine hand, and satisfies the desire of every living thing."

Our seasons of sunshine and rain are rich and glorious blessings too so our fields can yield crops for food. We are reminded in Matthew 5:45 "He maketh His sun to rise on the evil and on the good, and sended rain on the just and the unjust." With thanksgiving and praise we receive all these blessings of daily bread, which God gives in order for us to preserve our lives. In appreciation for our blessings we read in Psalm 128:1-2 "Blessed is everyone that fears the Lord; that walks in His ways. For you shall eat the labor of your hands; happy you shall be, and it shall be well with you."

God gives food to all people, even to the wicked; without them asking or being 'thankful'. We are reminded in 1 Timothy 6:6-8 "Godliness with contentment is great gain. For we have brought nothing into the world, and we will carry nothing out. Thereby having food and raiment let us be therein content."

Give thanks for all things, for that is well-pleasing unto the Lord! Because I was blessed with having grandparents living with us on the farm, I especially remember one grandmother referring to people not praying before sitting down to eat.

Grandma Ruth's comment: "If you don't pray before you eat, then you _do not_ deserve to eat what is set in front of you!" And, she meant it! Even if the supper menu consisted of Rabbit or Squirrel, and I can still visualize her standing, in her paralyzed state, at the stove frying grandpa's hunting successes.

And Forgive Us Our Trespasses, As We Forgive Those Who Trespass Against Us; "We daily sin much, and indeed deserve nothing by punishment". "My sin is ever before me". "Against Thee, and Thee alone have I sinned". Summoning up these short phrases from three different Bible passages is evident that we are sinful creatures, and that we cannot by our own reasoning, ability, determination, or power come before God feeling good about ourselves. It is absolutely because of the grace of God in our Lord and Savior Jesus that we can without merit and worthiness ask as in Psalm 51:1 "Be gracious to me, O God, according to Thy lovingkindness, and according unto the multitude of Thy tender mercies blot out my transgressions." Asking for and receiving forgiveness, we have peace with God, and St. Paul refers to it in Romans 5:1 "Therefore being justified by faith, we have peace with God through our Lord Jesus Christ."

Now we must with a sincere heart forgive those who have trespassed against us. How many times do we forgive others? Peter asked Jesus: "Lord, how many times shall my brother sin against me, and I forgive him? Up to seven times?" Jesus answered Peter: "I do not say to you up to seven times, but up to seventy times seven."

Could it be? That God will not forgive us, if we do not forgive others? I pray that we do not carry hatreds, animosities, grudges, and grievances toward others along with us to our graves. I pray, Dear Lord, let it not be so! Through being forgiven by God, and forgiving others we will be at peace with God, and have a good and clear conscience.

And Lead Us Not Into Temptation; Galatians 5:16-17 St Paul is very explicit in relating to us "I say, walk by the Spirit, and you will not carry out the desires of the flesh. For the flesh sets its desire against the Spirit, and the Spirit against the flesh for these are in opposition to one another, so that you do not do the things that you please." When the word 'flesh' is referred to, it is not the skin on our body, but our whole bodily being. Not one human being is immune to temptation, and in one way or another we have all experienced temptation.

Being tempted could as common as the air we breathe, because we were all born into sin, and all those yet unborn will be sinful. Even King David, a king chosen by God, found himself severely tempted, and his prayer entitled 'A Sinner's Prayer for Pardon' is found in Psalm 51. In verse 5 of that Psalm King David states out human condition, "Behold, I was brought forth in iniquity, and in sin did my mother conceive me." St Paul goes on in verses 19-21 warning us about the deeds of the flesh that can tempt us, and can keep us from inheriting The Kingdom of God. The world and all of its enticing avenues, and the devil telling us 'everybody is doing it'; after all this is the 21st Century. And there the devil talking to Eve: "Did God really say don't eat from that tree in the middle of the garden?" "You know if you eat from it; you're going to be like God." God was very explicit, but Eve didn't obey!

God didn't tempt Eve, and God won't tempt us, and we read in 1 Corinthians 10:13 "God is faithful, who will not allow you to be tempted beyond what you are able, but with the temptation God will provide the way of escape also, that you may be able to endure it."

God knows we are mere dust, and that we can easily be tempted, but we are His children through Holy Baptism, and God tells us in 2 Corinthians 12:9 "My grace is sufficient for thee; for My strength is made perfect in weakness."

But Deliver Us From Evil; Evil is what harms our body, our soul, our property, and our honor. Many times we hear the phrase, "Bad things can happen to good people." But bad things can happen to anyone. The bad is the evil when the devil permeates the minds of men, women, and children. The evil causes people much sorrow and total despair when their lives are threatened by deeds of sinful actions. Evil is never the will of God, but it has made this world a vale of tears. If we experience any evil, God will help us to endure and persevere. In Acts 14:22 St Paul affirms: "We must through much tribulation enter into the kingdom of God."

When evil/tribulations come, we can find comfort in hearing from Romans 8:28, "We know that all things work together for good to them that love God, to them who are called according to His purpose." And, again, in 2 Timothy 4:18, "The Lord shall deliver me from every evil work, and will preserve me unto His heavenly kingdom; to whom be glory for ever and ever." We pray that when our life on this earth ends, our Heavenly Father will graciously take us from this vale of tears to Himself in heaven.

For Thine is the kingdom, and the power, and the glory for ever and ever. Throughout Holy Scriptures we are constantly reminded of the Kingdom and the Power of God. In Chronicles 29:11 King David acknowledges: "Thine Oh Lord is the greatness and the power, and the glory, and the victory and the majesty. Indeed everything that is in the dominion Oh Lord and Thou dost exalt Thyself as Head over all".

At Jesus' Transfiguration He told Peter, James, and John that the Kingdom and the power of God would come through the Power of the Holy Spirit, and so it happened as we, again, refer to the account of Pentecost in the Book of Acts where the power of God became evident.

Jesus told the High Priest at His trial in Mark 14:62: "I am and you shall see the Son of Man sitting at the Right Hand of Power and coming with the clouds of heaven". We read the High Priest tore his clothes because he could not fathom who Jesus was and what Jesus had just promised. The High Priest called Jesus' promise blasphemy.

Some in today's culture are just "Living Their Dream" and they, like the High Priest, cannot fathom the Power of God, or that when God makes promises He will ultimately keep them! One day God's promise of His powerful day of judgement will come. We end **The Lord's Prayer** with an **AMEN.**

Through our daily 'prayer life' God will stay close to us when we stay close to Him. A hymn entitled "Just A Closer Walk With Thee" is sung by my autistic granddaughter as I accompany her on my piano. Jesus lovingly invites us in John 15:1-6: "Abide in Me and I will abide in you". Jesus refers to Himself as the vine, and we are the branches; branches not connected to the vine will die, will be cut away, and throw into the fire.

As we pray The Lord's Prayer and all of our prayers we know that they will be heard by our Father in Heaven, and we ask it in a beautiful hymn: "Oh Lord hear my prayer, Oh Lord hear my prayer; when I call answer me. Oh Lord hear my prayer, Oh Lord hear my prayer; come and listen to me."

We all have favorite prayers, and after praying the Lord's Prayer at night, I pray a prayer that my Aunt Linda taught me in German. The words in the German language rhyme beautifully, but not so in English. Aunt Linda told me to close my eyes and visualize what I was praying for, and asking God to send to my bedside.

I close my eyes and can still recite Aunt Linda's prayer in German.

Fourteen Angels (in English)
Evenings when I go to sleep, fourteen angels to stand by me;
two to my left side, two to my right side, two to my head, two to my feet,
two to cover me, two to wake me, and if I should die before I wake,
there will be two to carry me safely to heaven. Amen

Of course, Aunt Linda didn't need to close her eyes; Aunt Linda was blind.

While We Betray and Deny

To betray is a treacherous act of revealing something that should be kept a secret, or acting cruelly to someone. To deny is rejecting to acknowledge something or someone.

After praying in the garden, Jesus is subjected to betrayal and denial. Judas was right there without any reservations of betraying Jesus. Judas had told the Chief Priests when they gave him the 30 pieces of silver: "The one I kiss; it is He!"

Judas knew where the garden was, and he delivered Jesus into the hands of the Roman cohort, and officers from the Chief Priests and the Pharisees, and they were there with lanterns, torches, and weapons.

Jesus asked them: "Whom do you seek?" They answered: "Jesus the Nazarene." Jesus told them: "I am He."

And having told them they all fell to the ground. Jesus asked again: "Whom do you seek?" They answered again: "Jesus the Nazarene." Jesus replied again: "I told you that I am He; if therefore you seek Me, let these go their way." It is believed that Jesus was referring to His disciples when He said: "…let these go their way."

Peter, of course, being Peter drew his sword, struck a high priest's slave, and cut off his right ear. Jesus touching and healing the salve's ear told Peter: "Put the sword into the sheath; the cup which the Father has given Me, shall I not drink it?" Peter was always ready, willing, and a bit aggressive in defending his Lord. It was Peter that had told Jesus almost moments before: "I will never deny You; even if they all deny You; **Not me!**" What did Jesus tell Peter? "Before a cock crows today, you will have denied Me three times."

Jesus was bound and arrested and first brought to Annas, and then to Caiaphas the high priest. Peter had been following at a distance and coming to the courtyard of the high priest where a fire had been kindled, Peter sat among others outside. A certain servant-girl, seeing Peter in the firelight, and looking at him intently told the others: "This man was with Him too." Peter denied it saying: "Woman, I do not know Him." A little later, another saw Peter, and said: "You are one of them too." Peter answered: "Man, I am not." After an hour had passed another man pointed toward Peter and began to insist saying: "Certainly this man also was with Him, for he is a Galilean too." Peter angrily said: "Man, I do not know what you are talking about!" Immediately while Peter was still speaking, a cock crowed. The Lord tuned and looked at Peter, and Peter remembered *the word of the Lord.* Jesus had told Peter earlier: "Before a cock crows today, you will have denied Me three times." Peter immediately went out and wept bitterly.

Peter, of course, remembered too that Jesus had told him, and referring to him as a 'rock', and that it would be Peter's faith and confession of Peter's astounding statement: "You are The Christ!" on which Jesus would build His church. And Peter certainly remembered his words to Jesus: "Even if they all deny You. **Not me!**"

Was Peter's remorse so severe, and was he so ashamed of his denial that he couldn't show his face during the rest of Jesus' suffering and dying?

Perhaps Peter was standing at a distance watching in disbelief, but the Hold Scriptures make no mention of Peter's presence during the reminder of Jesus' trial or at His crucifixion.

Holy Scriptures does, however, make mention of Judas in detail. After seeing that Jesus had been condemned, Judas feeling remorse, returned the thirty pieces of silver to the chief priests and elders, and telling them: "I have sinned by betraying innocent blood." Their remark: "What is that to us? See to that yourself." Judas threw the pieces on the floor of the sanctuary, left, and went out and hung himself.

Judas betrayed the Lord, and even though Peter did deny the Lord miserably Peter did become what the Lord had foretold: Peter would become 'the rock' on which 'the church' was built.

We certainly need to note, again, that if either Judas or Peter had only remembered what Jesus had told them about Him rising up in three days, the circumstances would have been different; a whole lot different!

We know about Easter, and yet many times we do consciously deny our Lord, thereby denying ourselves a closer walk with our Lord and Savior by not being diligent in our prayer life or in worshiping. It is not that we do not believe. We do believe! But by not being diligent in prayer or worshiping we deny knowing our Lord, and it becomes evident as we interact with those we live and work with that we cannot sincerely acknowledge or witness our faith by how we conduct ourselves.

We may have been taught and instructed to conduct ourselves in a righteous and godly manner. But have we denied ourselves worldly desires, and do we live sensibly in our lifetime? We see words similar to that in Titus 2:11-15, "…to live sensibly, righteously, and godly in the present age."

When is the _present age_? Did it only pertain to the time when the book of Titus was written? Was the 'present age' during the Fifteenth Century? Could it have been one hundred years ago? Could it be this year? And, could it be one hundred years from now when someone else is reading these verses in Titus? Someone will always be living in the 'present age', and whatever year it may be, we can rest assure that there will always be 'worldly desires and vices' which are accepted socially, but will still, and will always be contrary to God's Holy Word.

We betray and deny our Loving Lord and Savior and the Holy Scriptures when we allow 'socially correct' practices to transform our lives. In 2 Timothy 3:1-15, we read concerning unholy living, and that we need to deny the power that is exerted on us from the world which offers and entices us daily to live ungodly lives. We need always be aware of those who profess to know God, but by their deeds they deny Him, and because of that they are detestable, disobedient, and worthless for any good deed. These are those who have then denied our Lord and Savior Jesus Christ.

Whenever 'the present age' or whomever is in the 'present age' we must be loving, do what is good and sensible, be just, devout, and self-controlling. We must hold on fast to the faithful word which is in accordance to the teaching of sound doctrine from the Holy Scriptures. We will always be looking for The Blessed Hope and the appearing of the glory of our great God and Savior Jesus Christ.

In Deuteronomy 8:11 we are warned that when we have built big houses, have enough to eat, and our wealth has increased we can deny and forget our God whom we should be thanking and praising for His blessings toward us. And in Proverbs 30:9 we are warned of having an abundance, as we read, "Lest I be full and deny Thee, and say "Who is the Lord?"

God can also be denied in the face of adversity, and perhaps we blame God for our condition be it poverty or a grave illness. The book of Job describes the horrible tragedies that Job endured. Job lost his children, his wealth, and finally his health. Even Job's wife could not understand why Job did not and would not blame God, or deny God his worship and praise. From Job a beautiful hymn was written, and we sing it many times, and especially at Easter; "I Know That My Redeemer Lives".

Let us never forget what Jesus assures us in Matthew 10:32, "Everyone therefore who shall confess Me, I will confess before My Father who is in heaven. But, whoever shall deny Me before men, I will also deny him before My Father who is in heaven."

While We Protest

In a protest individuals want it 'Their Way'! And, they want to be heard!

Jesus' appearing before the Sanhedrin started with torture, but a brutal protest by the Council of the church elders accelerated to a full-fledged protest by the multitude before Pilate with shouts of "Crucify Him! Crucify Him!" We read in the Holy Scriptures that before the Sanhedrin in the Council of the elders, the arresting officers began beating and mocking Jesus. They blindfolded Him, spit on Him, slapped Him in the face, and asked sneeringly: "Prophesy, who is the one who hit you?"

Jesus was asked by the council: "If you are the Christ, tell us." Jesus told them: "If I tell you, you will not believe. But from now on the Son of Man will be seated at the right hand of the power of God." They asked: "Are you the Son of God?" Jesus answered truthfully: "Yes, I am." The Council, and the high priest tearing his clothes, called Jesus' answer blasphemy, and they condemned Him to be deserving of death. They bound Jesus, and brought Jesus to Pilate.

Jesus' first appearance before Pilate didn't go very well for the Council of the Elders. The whole body of them began to accuse Jesus telling Pilate that Jesus had called Himself Christ, a King. Pilate asked Jesus: "Are You the King of the Jews?" Jesus answered: "It is as you say." Of course Pilate didn't have a problem with Jesus' answer, because Pilate wasn't a Jew, Pilate was a Roman. Pilate told the Chief Priests: "I find no fault in this man." Finding out

that Jesus was a Galilean, and under Herod's jurisdiction Pilate sent Jesus to Herod.

Now Herod was pleased, because he had wanted to see Jesus for a long time, and he was hoping he would see some miraculous signs performed by Jesus. Herod's questioning didn't satisfy the Chief Priests and scribes, because Jesus didn't answer Herod's questions. The Chief Priests and scribes kept accusing Jesus vehemently which angered Herod. Therefore, Herod and his soldiers treated Jesus with contempt and sent Jesus back to Pilate.

Before Pilate a second time, Pilate's wife came to him and told him: "Have nothing to do with that righteous man; for last night I suffered greatly in a dream because of Him." And now, again, before Pilate the number of spectators had become larger than Jesus' first appearance before Pilate, and finally we read that there are multitudes. Pilate came out, again, telling the Chief Priests, and the crowds: "I am bringing Him out to you, that you may know I find no fault in Him."

It was customary that at this time to release one prisoner, and a notorious murderer named Barabbas was being held. Pilate brought out Jesus and Barabbas, and asked the multitude which one of these two would they want released.

At that moment, Pilate was Jesus' only defense, and Pilate believed that the multitude would let Jesus go free, but we read that it was the Chief Priests and elders that persuaded and incited the multitudes to ask for Barabbas's release. Pilate asked: "Then what shall I do with Jesus who is called Christ?" The multitude shouted: "Let Him be crucified!"

Pilate realized that he wasn't accomplishing anything, and because a riot was starting, he took water and washed his hands in front of the multitude, and said: "I am innocent of this Man's blood; see to that yourselves." The multitude shouted: "His blood be on us and on our children". Barabbas was released, and

Jesus was handed over to them to be crucified. Jesus was scourged mercilessly, soldiers wove a crown of thorns, and placed it on His head. They brought a robe, and putting it on Him they mocked Him saying: "Hail king of the Jews." They placed a reed in His hand, then took it from Him and beat Him over the head. The crown of thrones must have punched holes in Jesus' head even deeper. They continued mocking Jesus and striking Him with blows to His face.

Did the multitude of protestors get their way? They certainly did, and the Chief Priests and elders inciting the multitude got their way too. This Jesus who proclaimed to be King of the Jews would now be put to 'silence' once and for all.

We need to understand something about the Chief Priests and elders. They wanted an earthly king; namely like King David. A king that would get them out of the 'grips' of the Romans, because the Jewish People were living under Roman law. Their own earthly king would give them their freedom from Rome. The Chief Priests and elders knew all the prophesies of the Old Testament, but they could not comprehend that Jesus was the 'king' they had been waiting for. They did not accept Jesus as their Lord and Savior thereby being their Heavenly King.

Jesus being True God, and His divine birth, life, death, resurrection, and Ascension was predicted throughout the Old Testament by the prophets, and was totally and ultimately fulfilled by Jesus Himself as it is recorded in the New Testament.

Yet many are still protesting, for a 'silence' to what the Holy Scriptures reveals so precisely and truthfully. We protest as to what we don't agree with in the Holy Scriptures. We want some lifestyles removed, because they are now politically and socially correct, and no longer relevant by today's standards. And so there is a protest going on in today's society, because many individuals can no longer accept the Authority of Holy Scriptures!

There are those who protest by wanting all Christian symbols removed from public facilities and banning Nativity Scenes because they have now become objectionable to some religious or atheistic groups.

Persecution is a form of protesting; Christian civilians and Christian missionaries are put to death for their belief. We must pray that God would ease their suffering, and forgive their enemies as Jesus forgave His enemies in His words from the cross: "Father forgive them for they do not know what they are doing." Have we ever thought about preparing ourselves for bodily and physical persecution here in America?

It is human nature to protest, and we can protest, too, by remaining faithful in our faith to our Lord and Savior Jesus Christ! We protest in living our lives in a godly manner! Our life is a gift from God, and the way we live our life is our gift to God. We protest peacefully with our prayers, and our voting! God sees our protesting, and we pray we will always protest to the Glory of God!! And, we protest in the words of a beautiful hymn:

"Stand Up Stand Up For Jesus"
As soldiers of the cross, Lift high the royal banner; it must not suffer loss. From victory unto victory His army He shall lead. Till every foe is vanquished, and Christ is Lord indeed.

While We Carry

We can't even begin to imagine the brutality that our Dear Savior endured as we see Him carry the cross.

And where were the disciples during all of this? Had they abandoned Jesus or were the eleven remaining disciples in hiding somewhere in Jerusalem? Did they see the mocking, the torture, and the agony that their Lord had just experienced? Did they hear the rioting multitude crying: "Crucify Him!"

Were the disciples watching, now, as the heavy cross bar of the cross was laid on Jesus for Him to carry it to the place where the crucifixion was to take place?

Did the disciples see the man who had come in from the country? A man named Simon of Cyrene who probably wanted to see what was going on. Perhaps he had heard the shouts of an angry mob way out in the country. Were the disciples watching as the soldiers took the cross from Jesus, and laid it on Simon to carry it behind Jesus? Perhaps the disciples were disguised, and in the multitude that was following Jesus. We know there were some women in that multitude that were mourning and feeling sorrowful for Jesus.

Jesus felt more compassion for them in telling them: "Daughters of Jerusalem, stop weeping for Me, but weep for yourselves and for your children." And Jesus added: "Then they will begin to say to the mountains, 'fall on us' and to the hills, 'cover us'". What did Jesus exactly mean by these statements? Jesus foretold God's judgement on the world, and that people would attempt to escape God's judgement. We wonder whether the sin of mankind can become so intense, that when the end of the world does come, will people really believe that they can escape God's judgement? Would that not be a pitiful scenario? Can we not comprehend the fact that all mankind starting with Adam and Eve, to the present, and into the future will not and cannot escape God's judgement?

Now we see our Dearest Savoir so brutally beaten, walking in front of His cross, and taking upon Himself God's fierce judgement of all our sins, infirmities, imperfections, and diseases, and carrying them all to the cross for us. Seeking God's forgiveness, being repentant, and believing in our Savior Jesus Christ is our 'perfect escape' from God's fierce judgement from every sin we have ever committed.

In 2 Corinthians 4 St Paul brings to mind how we are afflicted in many ways, even having our own crosses to bear, but we are not forsaken, struck down or destroyed. We can day by day _carry_ in our bodies the dying of Jesus and living a life that we are called for to live according to God's purpose for us.

Also, in 2 Corinthians 12 starting with verse 7, we read that even St Paul had a 'cross to bear' he referred to it as a 'thorn in the flesh', and he asked God to take it away three times, but God replied: "My grace is sufficient for you, for power is perfected in weakness." St Paul concurred: "Most gladly, therefore, I will rather boast about my weakness, that the power of Christ may dwell in me."

How does one boast in weakness? Is our faith strong enough to accept a cross that we may be carrying? And, is God's grace sufficient for us? Jesus did say: "Take up your cross and follow Me." Jesus knows our every weakness, sees our condition, and He knows how He will respond to our heartfelt requests as we _carry_ everything to God in prayer and in the words of a beautiful hymn.

"Take Up Your Cross," The Savior said, "If you would my disciple be; forsake the past, and come this day, and humbly follow after me. Take up your cross, And follow Christ, Nor think till death to lay it down; For only those who bear the cross may hope to wear a golden crown."

Now, let's follow Jesus to Calvary.

While We Hear

We aren't exactly certain how Pilate 'pulled this off', but Pilate did take a stand, and did have a final word for the Chief Priests and elders, and perhaps it had something to do with what his wife had shared more explicitly with him from her dream. Pilate wrote an inscription and put it on the cross. It read: "JESUS THE NAZARENE, THE KING OF THE JEWS", and it was written in Hebrew, Latin, and Greek. The Chief Priests told Pilate: "Do not write, The King of the Jews, but write that He said He was the king of the Jews." Pilate answered: "What I have written, I have written!"

I remember when growing up, and in observance of Good Friday, all stores and business' closed at 12:00 noon, and didn't open again until 3:00 p.m. These three hours gave employees the opportunity to attend Worship Services.

During these three hours depicting Jesus' crucifixion we hear Jesus' final words, and witness the horribleness of His suffering and dying on the cross.

"Father forgive them, for they do not know what they are doing."

Jesus prayer was sincere and forgiving, as He asked God to forgive His enemies; the very people that were so responsible for His suffering, and now having nailed Him to the cross. We can't even imagine having such brutal enemies, but many innocent people have experienced tragic events in their lives. Possibly some of us have been mistreated by others, and possibly we have done some mistreating of our own to others. When we hear Jesus forgiving, how can we not want to forgive in order that we want to be forgiven for what we had done? Even those small minutiae annoyances that some people have caused us? Ah, yes, even those should not be held against others.

"My God, My God, why hast Thou forsaken Me?"

Was Jesus' suffering so intense, that in His human state He was truly asking? Did God really forsake Him? Have we ever asked God similar questions? "Where are you Lord?" "Oh Dear Lord, how can this be happening to me?" Have illness, issues in our family, financial problems, and pressures at work, or loss of work been so overwhelming that we cannot comprehend a foreseeable escape from our burden? I have experienced all of the above, and I can truthfully say that I have prayerfully asked God for help, and in God's 'Good Time'; not my timetable all prayers were answered, and some may still be waiting to be answered. Again, in God's own time.

"Woman, behold your son. Son behold your mother."

Now we learn that one disciple, John, is mentioned standing at the foot of the cross comforting Jesus' mother Mary. What must dear Mary be feeling? Mary too, like the disciple John standing there beside her, had forgotten about Jesus fore-telling His death and Resurrection message. All Mary could think about was her Baby lying in the manger, and was now bleeding and hanging above her on a cross.

There is a beautiful and emotional Christmas Carol entitled: "Mary Did You Know?" The carol keeps asking Mary questions, and one question which is so emotional is: "Mary did you know when you kiss your Baby, you are kissing the face of God?" Another question is: "Mary did you know that your Baby Boy has come to save you too?" I have sung that carol several times at Christmas Concerts, and I still tear-up. And from that day on, the disciple John took Mary as his own mother, and Mary took the disciple John as her own son.

"Truly I say to you; today you shall be with Me in paradise."

Two criminals were crucified with Jesus; one of each side of Jesus. The one wanted to be free from his sentence to die; he must have heard of Jesus and some miracles that Jesus had done. He wanted to see Jesus perform a miracle now, and he didn't just ask, but almost demanded: "If you are the Christ, save Yourself and us." This criminal wanted a 'free ticket' from punishment that he apparently deserved. The ironic thing is that Jesus could have done just that!! Jesus being God could have stunned everyone standing at the foot of His cross, and miraculously Jesus could have walked away.

If Jesus had done that, He would have walked away from us!

St Paul tells us in 2 Corinthians 5:21, "He made Him who knew no sin to be sin on our behalf, that we might become the righteousness of God in Him." Jesus was God's remedy for sin; our sin, Jesus being God remained on that cross of His own free will to atone for our sins. The criminal who wanted to see a miracle and have his freedom didn't understand that, and he could have owed up to his sins as the other criminal did. Now the other criminal, perhaps having heard of Jesus, too, but never accepted Him until now rebukes his counterpart, and tells him: "We're guilty, but this Man has done no wrong." Then in pure repentance he asked Jesus: "Remember me when You get into Your kingdom." And, Jesus being True God, could look into this criminal's heart, see his repentance, and told him: "Truly I say to you; today you shall be with Me in paradise".

Pure repentance can be asked by anyone at any moment during any situation when an individual accepts Jesus as Lord and Savior. A prayerful hymn with an almost haunting melody with only two phrases is frequently sung in Worship Services. "Jesus, remember me, when You come into Your kingdom. Jesus remember me when You come Your kingdom."

"I Thirst."

In Jesus' human state, He is thirsty. We read that a sponge of sour wine was placed on a branch of hyssop, and raised to Jesus' mouth. Would this sour wine quench Jesus' thirst or, for that matter, anyone's thirst? Or was it just another way of mocking Him?

In John Chapter 4 we hear Jesus asking a Samaritan woman at a well: "Give Me a drink." The woman was curious, because Jews and Samaritans had no dealings with each other, and she wondered why a Jew was asking her a Samaritan for a drink of water. The chapter goes to tell us that Jesus knew she was in need of Him as her Savior, and Him would be her "Living Water" because of her lifestyle. Do we, because of our lifestyles, need Jesus as our "Living Water"? Do we thirst for forgiveness as we look up to the cross? When we look to Jesus, and say: "I thirst," Our Lord and Savior will offer us "Living Water" too.

"Father into Your Hands, I commit My Spirit"

Did Jesus know that His suffering would almost be over? Yes, Jesus knew that His Father's will would be done, as it had been in His life, in His suffering, and, now, in His death, and He was committing His earthly body and God's Holy Will into God's Holy Hands. Have we fully committed and entrusted our lives to God? Verses in Psalm 37 speak of the security of those who 'Trust in the Lord and do good', 'Delight yourself in the Lord', 'Commit your way to the Lord', 'Dwell in the land and cultivate faithfulness'. 'The salvation of the righteous is from the Lord; He is their strength in time of trouble. And the Lord helps them and delivers them from the wicked, and saves them, because they take refuge in Him'.

How will we say: "Father, into Your hands I commit my spirit" when death is awaiting us? A beautiful hymn comes to mind: "Precious Lord take my hand, lead me on, let me stand. I am tired, I am weak, I am worn. Through the storm, through the night, lead me to the light. Take my hand Precious Lord, lead me home."

Jesus said: "It Is Finished" and bowing His head, breathing His last breath, Jesus gave up His Spirit which signified that His Divine Work of Salvation had been ultimately and perfectly completed for the entire world; past, present, and future generations to come!

What is happening now as we see Jesus hanging and dead? The Jews did not want the three bodies remaining on the crosses on the Sabbath, and they asked Pilate that their legs be broken, and taken down. First the Romans soldiers did break the legs of the two men that been crucified with Jesus, but when they came to Jesus, and seeing that He was already dead, they did not break His legs, and piecing Jesus' side they saw water and blood flowing from His side. This, too, was revealed from Holy Scriptures in John 19:36, "Not a bone of Him shall be broken." The piercing of Jesus' side was foretold in Zechariah 12:10, "They shall look on Him Whom they have pierced."

In the thick darkness that had fallen over the city, the earth began to shake, and the soldiers and the centurion who had been keeping guard near the cross suddenly became frightened, and exclaimed: "Truly this was the Son of God!" What many standing there did not realize was that, at this very moment, the veil of the temple was being torn in two; from top to bottom.

In Exodus chapters 25 to 27 God had given Moses specific instructions how to build the tabernacle, which included multiple curtains, and veils. Only the High Priests could enter behind the veils to worship God; the people were not allowed to enter what was considered 'the Holy of Holies."

The religious custom continued throughout the Old Testament, so even in the temple in Jerusalem there was a veil, and until now only a High Priest could enter keeping the people separated from God.

That day which we call Good Friday, our loving and almighty God changed all of that! The torn veil represented that Jesus' divine suffering and death for our sins was God's intervention for reconciling Himself with all of mankind.

We are no longer separated from God!

The Bible doesn't tell us how the Chief Priests and the Jewish leaders reacted when they learned that the veil had been torn in two.

We weren't there to _hear_ the last seven words of Jesus, but we can read them from the pages of Holy Scripture, we will hear them in our Lenten Worship Services, and we will listen to them with our hearts.

Our journey of walking with Jesus to His cross can leave us sorrowful for our Dear Lord and Savior's suffering and dying, and we find we have had a much closer walk with Jesus that we have ever had before, and looking up at Him we tremble, and we can answer "Yes" to the hymn: "Where You There" when they crucified my Lord?

My mother's favorite hymn sung during the Passion Season was: "The Old Rugged Cross": "On a hill far away stood an old rugged cross, the emblem of suffering and shame; And I love that old cross where the dearest and best for a world of lost sinners was slain. So I'll cherish that cross, till my trophies at last I lay down; I will cling to the old rugged cross, and exchange it someday for a crown."

A secret disciple of Jesus named Joseph of Arimathea fearing the Jews, asked Pilate for permission to take Jesus' body. With the help of a Jewish leader named Nicodemus, who too had secretly come to know Jesus, they took Jesus' body bound it with linens and spices as was the burial custom of the Jews, to a garden and placed Jesus' body in a new tomb belonging to Joseph of Arimathea. A large stone was placed at the entrance of the tomb.

The Chief Priests and Pharisees still had some concerns about Jesus, and they remembered Jesus' words about 'rebuilding the temple in three days', and they feared that Jesus' disciples would come, take His body, and then say that Jesus had arisen. Going to Pilate the Chief Priests and Pharisees asked for guards to be posted at the tomb, and Pilate granted them their wishes to secure the tomb with guards.

While in the tomb, Jesus was exalted, His work of redemption was confirmed as was His entry into glory, and this signifies that Jesus being True God, and because He is True God, Jesus had one more 'mission' to accomplish! Jesus victoriously descended into hell, and triumphantly defeated sin, death, and power of Satan. We read in 1 John 3:6, "For this purpose the Son of God was manifested, that He might destroy the works of the devil."

One may ask why this account of Jesus defeating Satan is never seen in any Biblical movie. Could it be too terrifying? Beginning in November each year, The Sights & Sounds Theatre in Branson, MO present a beautiful and powerful live-production of "The Christmas Story" which ends with Jesus' Resurrection, but before the Resurrection, the theatre does vividly depict Jesus defeating Satan. And, it is extremely terrifying! First the audience is almost mesmerized, and then some sincere joyfulness 'of victory' resounds throughout the massive theatre.

It is difficult to find words to describe how impeccable the theatre is in reenacting the Resurrection, and tissues begin to appear as one watches the magnificent beauty and splendor of Jesus' Glorious Resurrection. Leaving the theatre with tearful eyes, I felt certain that Mary's tears upon seeing Jesus in the garden were of a much larger magnitude.

When we attend Worship Services during the Passion Season our faith in Christ deepens, and our hope and assurance that the 'agony of the cross' that Jesus endured for us has now become the **'Glory of the Cross'** for us.

With joyfulness we can share with others that we know what is really finished! Our eternal death sentence!!

He Is Risen!
He is risen Indeed!
Alleluia!

In the light of dawn on this first day of week, we are looking beyond the garden, and we see three empty crosses. Then think about Mary Magdalene, Joanna, and Mary the mother of James coming toward the tomb. The women are carrying prepared spices and perfumes to anoint Jesus' body. Perhaps suddenly they asked themselves: "What only were we thinking?" Who will roll away the stone for us from the entrance of the tomb?" Coming closer, they saw that the stone had been rolled away, and two angels in white sitting, one at the head and one at the feet where Jesus' body was lying. The women were terrified, and an angel tells them: "Do not be afraid." "Why do seek the living One among the dead?" Mary, still somewhat skeptical, is seen weeping, and turning she sees Jesus, but she does not recognize Him. Jesus asks: "Woman, why are you weeping?" Mary replies: "They have taken my Lord, and I do not know where they have laid Him." Mary thinking him to be a gardener asks: "Sir, if you have carried Him away, tell me where you have laid Him".

Jesus softly spoke her name: "Mary", and she recognized Him, and said to Him in Hebrew, "Rabboni" (which means Teacher).

Can we even begin to imagine how quickly Mary's tears of sorrow were now turning to tears of joy? Jesus said to her, "Do not hold Me, for I have not yet ascended to my Father, but go to my brethren and Peter, and say to them, I am ascending to my Father and your Father, to my God and your God." With that joy Mary ran with haste to tell the disciples: "I have seen the Lord!"

We ask why did the Lord specifically name 'Peter' when He said: "Go and tell my brethren and Peter"? Peter, the one and the same who had so bitterly wept after his denial of his Lord and Savior. The Peter that the Lord referred as 'a rock on which His church would be built on'. The Peter that the Lord already knew would be addressing the crowds in Jerusalem on Pentecost for the 'outpouring of The Holy Spirit'. We read that Peter was one of the first disciples to run to the empty tomb after hearing Mary telling them that she had seen the Lord.

That same Peter would have to see for himself, and we would almost be able to visualize Peter running toward the tomb, and then briskly walking into the tomb, carefully casing it out, taking note of the burial linens, walking out, and then even going back inside for a second look.

Peter can now be seen rushing out of the tomb, and suddenly one can see his excitement, and an exuberant smile from ear to ear, and there is no doubt in Peter's mind **what had happened!** With two thumbs up, and an expression of 'today', Peter loudly exclaimed:

"YES!"

And we Exclaim:
He is risen! He Is Risen Indeed! Alleluia!

Easter is a 'message of peace' as we sing a beautiful hymn entitled: "In the Cross of Christ I Glory" towering over the wrecks of time. All the light of sacred story gathers round its head sublime. When the woes of life o'er take me, hopes deceive and fears annoy. Never shall the cross forsake me; lo it glows with peace and joy"

"Peace be with you" is what Jesus told His disciples on Easter evening when He came to them where they were hiding in fear.

We, too, many times are fearful, but because of our crucified Lord and Savior's death, Resurrection, and Ascension Christ wants to replace our fear with peace knowing that He atoned for our sins, and He continuously comes to us in His Word and Holy Sacrament.

After Easter we have the "Peace the passes all human understanding as we keep our hearts and minds in Christ Jesus."

A Blessed Easter and God's Blessings to all!

In Conclusion

Does the Resurrection of our Lord and Savior inspire us to live as 'Resurrected Christians' after Easter? Can our faith withstand living in this society in which secularism is ever present, and which in many ways contradicts the very Authority of Holy Scripture?

Jesus spoke many parables in His teaching while alive, but the one we find in Matthew 25 is most significant in how we live our lives on a daily basis as we await and watch for our Lord's Second Coming. Not to wait in fear, but to keep our faith burning brightly, and not allowing ourselves to become conformed to living our lives by todays secular standards that most certainly contradict the Authority of Holy Scripture.

The Ten Virgins: All ten virgins were Christians. All ten knew that the Lord (the bridegroom) would be coming to take them to their Eternal Rest (the feast). Five wise virgins kept their faith (oil lanterns) well lite. Five unwise virgins left their faith (oil lanterns) flicker, and were almost becoming extinguished.

Are we virgins that keep our faith burning brightly before others in a way that reflect our love for God, and our love for others? Are we faithful in worship, in our prayer life, and most importantly do we hold the Authority of Hold Scripture sacred in how we live our lives?

Are we virgins that find worship not important any longer? Has our prayer life ceased, and are we allowing ourselves to being conformed to what is becoming 'politically or society correct'? Do we find ourselves even doubting the Authority of Holy Scriptures by asking: "Did God really mean that?" Or do we argue: "There are references in the Bible that aren't relevant any longer, because they don't pertain to today's standards!"

Sadly! There are some clergy that have allowed their faith (oil lanterns) to flicker, because they no longer hold the Authority of Holy Scriptures sacred.

No one knows when the Lord (the bridegroom) will appear. Today the Lord may call us from our death bed, a car accident, or an act of violence. The Final Hour of Judgement is known by no one except by God! Jesus said: "Only My Father knows the hour and the day." The Bible tells us it will come as a thief coming by night.

God does promise that we will see the heavens open with the power of God, with a multitude of angels, and our Lord and Savior descending on the clouds. In 1 Thessalonians 4:16 we read: "The dead in Christ will rise first." But the Lord's second coming on Judgement Day will most certainly find many that will still be alive; going to work, going to school, cooking dinner, going shopping, or perhaps watching and enjoying an indoor or an outdoor sports event.

How well our faith (our lanterns) will be burning brightly when our Lord calls us to our Eternal Rest is ALL ON US!

Are we 'Resurrected Christians'? Will we be ready to enter Eternal Rest with our Lord who lived, who suffered, who was crucified and died for our sins, was buried, defeated Satan (and all he stands for), arose from the dead, and ascended into heaven where He is seated at the Right Hand of God? And, I pray we all can answer: "YES!" Our Lord and Savior did all of that for us, and He Has a Blessed New Heaven and New Earth prepared and waiting for us to enjoy with Him in a Glorious Forever!

I prayerfully encourage all to read the very last chapter in the Bible: Revelations 22; only 21 verses. It is beautiful and profound, and it clearly emphasis keeping the Authority of Holy Scripture sacred, and a Christian's Eternal Rest.

When we can't even begin to imagine God's unfathomable love for us, we need only to read John 3:16-17, "For God so loved the world, that He gave His only begotten Son, that whoever believes in Him should not perish, but have eternal life. For God did not send the Son into the world to condemn the world, but that the world should be saved through Him."

About the Author

Since Patricia wrote *While Grandma Is Sleeping*, she has had her own crosses to bear. While her one son was becoming weaker from Brain Cancer, and still is, her other son went to his Eternal Rest after a short battle with Colon Cancer. Patricia recalls a verse in one of the sympathy cards she received came from Proverbs 10:7: "The memory of the righteous is a blessing." The memory of her dear son brings her much comfort, but her questions and her tears she gives to God.

God understands Patricia's questions, and sympathizes with her tears. In Psalm 56:8 she reads: "Thou has taken account of the path I am on, Put my tears in Thy bottle." But the path she is on, cannot cause her to lose her faith, as that would be disastrous for her soul.

What does St Paul ask in Romans 8:35? "Who shall separate us from the love of Christ? Shall tribulation, or distress, or persecution, or famine, or nakedness, or peril, or sword?"

And further in verse 37 we read: "But in all things we overwhelmingly conquer through Him who loved us. For I am convinced that neither death, nor life, nor angels, nor principalities, nor things present, nor things to come, nor powers, nor height, nor depth shall be able to separate us from the love of God, which is in Christ Jesus our Lord."

Patricia relates that the Lord is her Rock and her Refuge, and the Joy of the Lord is her Strength. She relates from Proverbs 17:22, "A joyful heart is good medicine; But a broken spirit dries up the bones." She prays that all those who are burdened with crosses find Love, Peace, and God's Blessings.

Reviews

"I enjoyed reading *While Walking To The Cross* and found it spiritually based."
    —Rev. Greg Douthwaite - Retired

"In having the pleasure in reading Patricia Frank's *While Walking To The Cross*, I found, as in her previous book *While Grandma Is Sleeping*, this book, also, is based entirely on Holy Scripture. *While Walking To The Cross* is a beautiful expression of Patricia's faith. In God's love and care."
    —Rev. Elaine Gerth - Retired
    Ministering for The Lord
    Past pastor for 17 years at Our Saviour's Lutheran Church, Iron Ridge, WI
    Past interim pastor for 2 years at County Line Lutheran Church, Markesan, WI

"Dear Patricia,
Kay and I were pleased that you asked us to review your new book *While Walking To The Cross*. It was a pleasure and edifying to read what you wrote. I am sure it will be a blessing to others as they read it."
    —Pastor Emeritus Roger and Kay Zehms